Trilochan Das, Dhanna Jat and the Stone Idols

Adapted from a story by Sant Ram Singh Ji, August 15, 2015

Illustrated by Carlos Brito

Trilochan Das, Dhanna Jat and the Stone Idols

Trilochan Das, Dhanna Jat and
the Stone Idols was originally told in a Satsang by
Sant Ram Singh Ji on August 15, 2015 at
Channasandra Ashram, near Bangalore, India.

Special thanks to those who critiqued and reviewed the story:
Bernard Daniel, Richard and Sharon Malarich.
Their suggestions have made the adult story
more appropriate for children.

Translated by Ashok Shinkar
Transcribed by Ali Czernin, Geoff Halstead, & Harvey Rosenberg

Carlos Brito's vibrant use of color and his fun,
whimsical characters bring the words of the story to life
making it a work of art,
while adding joy to our hearts and beauty to our souls.
Thank you, dear Carlos.

ISBN-13: 978-1-942937-15-9

Published by
www.gojollybooks.com
Go Jolly Books
74 Gem Ln., Sandpoint, ID 83864

FIRST EDITION, GO JOLLY BOOKS, First Printing 2016
10 9 8 7 6 5 4 3 2 1 Printed in the U.S.A.

Trilochan Das, Dhanna Jat and the Stone Idols

Adapted from a story by Sant Ram Singh Ji, August 15, 2015

GO JOLLY BOOKS

INTRODUCTION

In January, 2014, at Channasandra Ashram located near Bangalore, India, I asked Sant Ram Singh Ji if I could take stories He told in Satsang and publish them as books.

Although I don't recall His exact words, He said yes. Then He told me to make sure the books were for children. To me that meant I could substitute difficult Hindi translated words geared to adults with words more suitable for children without losing Sant Ram Singh's meaning.

With His Limitless Grace, reviewers of the first three books have told us we have made the books easier for children to understand.

Trilochan Das, Dhanna Jat, and The Stone Idols is a story that demonstrates how a devotee should do his or her devotion. It's a beautiful story of love and faith and the vibrant, whimsical color combinations and characters truly make the story come alive. We hope you enjoy it.

Radhaswami,
Harvey Rosenberg

Trilochan Das, Dhanna Jat and the Stone Idols

Adapted from a story by Sant Ram Singh Ji, August 15, 2015

This book is dedicated to Sant Ram Singh Ji,

a Sant Mat Master Who showers His Limitless Grace,

Unconditional Love and Acceptance of us

every single moment of our lives

as He attempts to make us like Himself.

He is our True Friend and a Living Master.

Dhanna Jat was a devotee who lived in a hut in the Punjab and earned his income as a laborer. He practiced a lot of meditation and had been Graced to see the Radiant Form of His Master within.

Dhanna Jat lived with his grandmother in a town where each year a family guru named Trilochan Das visited. Trilochan Das and each family would do various rituals together and as payment, the families made offerings to the guru.

Although Dhanna Jat had frugal earnings, he was very devoted and connected to the Sound Current within. He wanted to enlighten Trilochan Das, so he also invited Trilochan Das to his house to perform rituals.

When Trilochan Das came to his house, he opened his bag and removed all his false deities. These were small idols of various gods and goddesses. Before serving or consuming food, people typically place food in front of the idols as the ritual, which is what Trilochan Das did.

Then, Trilochan Das, Dhanna Jat and his grandmother ate. After the meal, when Trilochan Das was packing his idols and preparing to leave, Dhanna Jat asked him to give him one deity, one idol so that he could also worship that idol for the year until Trilochan Das returned.

Trilochan Das was not very keen to give him an idol, so Dhanna Jat said, "Okay, I won't keep it for the year. You take it when you leave our town."

Trilochan Das replied, "Okay, I will give you one idol when I leave."

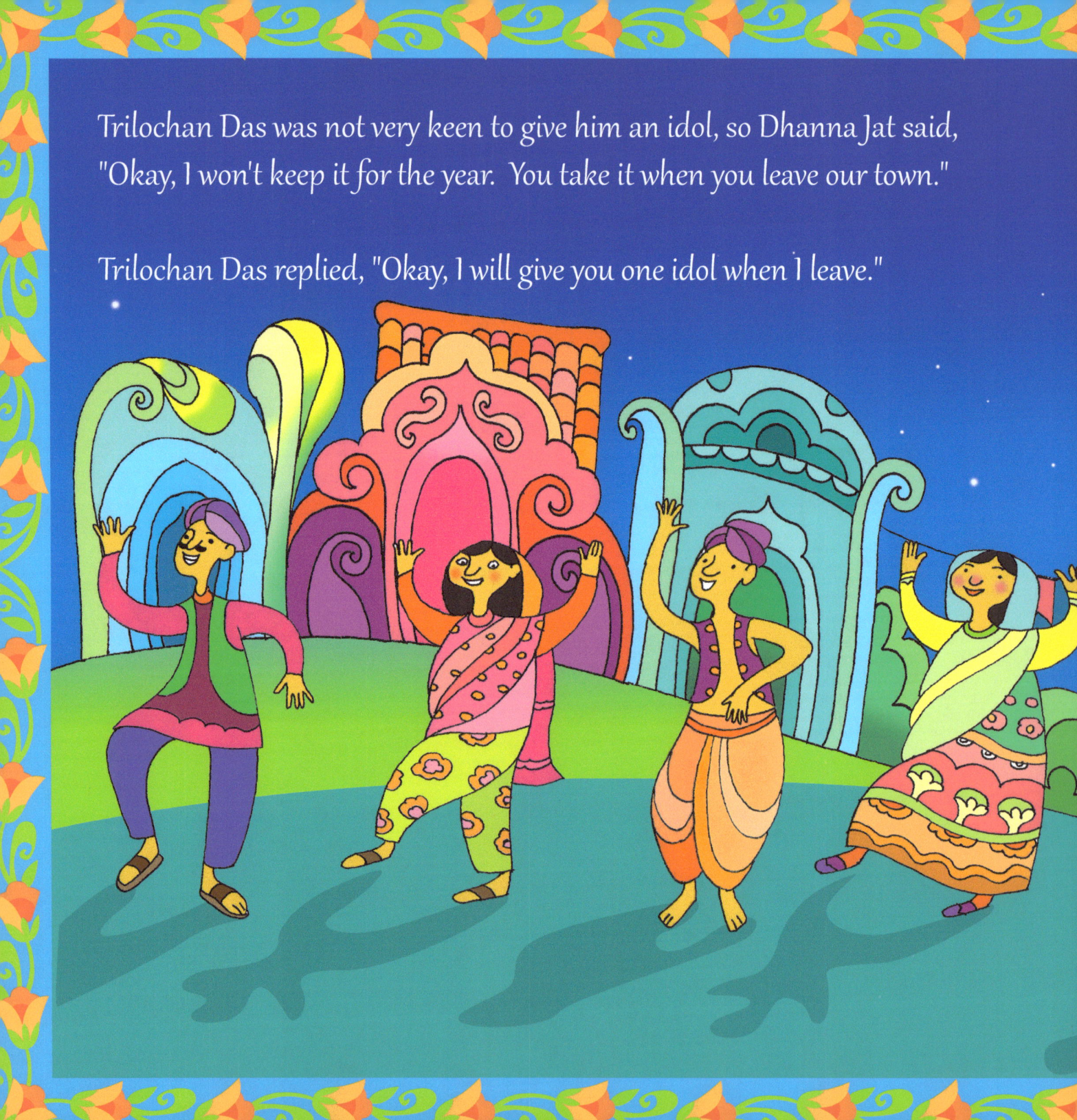

Trilochan Das continued visiting each family in town. Finally, when the festivities were completed, when all the food had been served, Trilochan Das received payment for his rituals and began preparing to depart.

As he was loading his cart, Dhanna Jat came running to him and said, "You promised to give me one idol when you leave."

Although Trilochan Das had said he would give Dhanna Jat an idol, he had no intention of actually giving him an idol. Instead, he looked around for a small pebble or stone, something to give to Dhanna Jat. But in the Punjab, the land is so fertile that you seldom find stones there. So there was nothing.

Finally, Trilochan Das found a dropping of a goat, which he gave to Dhanna Jat and said, "Look, this is a ling, it's like Shiva. It's a deity. Pray to it, worship it, and use it to do the ritual."

On receiving the ling, Dhanna Jat bowed towards Trilochan Das and said, "Thank you very much. You have blessed me with this deity."

Then Trilochan Das told him how to worship.

He said, "Place the ling on a plain white cloth. Worship and pray to the ling. Give the ling a little food, and after doing that, you eat your food."

Dhanna Jat listened closely to the instructions, then went up to the attic, laid a plain white cloth on the floor, and placed the ling on the cloth.

When his grandmother gave him a plate of dal, rice and roti, Dhanna Jat offered some to the deity, to the ling, saying, "Take this food. Only after you eat, I will eat."

Dhanna Jat sat comfortably and waited for the deity to eat.
But the ling ate nothing.

Finally, after waiting a long time, he gave his food to a cow.

Dhanna Jat didn't understand why the ling ate none of the food he placed before it, but for five days he continued to offer the deity food. Yet day after day, Dhanna Jat ended up giving his food to the cow when the food for the deity remained on the cloth, uneaten.

After not eating for five days, Dhanna Jat lost a lot of weight, became frail and weak. God Himself, Who knows everything, felt that if Dhanna Jat didn't eat soon, he would die.

On the sixth day of Dhanna Jat not eating, God Himself manifested and accepted the offering of two rotis which Dhanna gave Him. After eating one roti, Dhanna Jat asked God Almighty, "What about me?"

Then He offered that second roti to Dhanna, who happily ate it, which gave him faith in the ling.

Whenever Dhanna Jat was given food by his grandmother, he would go to the attic, offer some to God and then eat what remained.

After a few days in which God was eating like this, He felt, "I am eating his food. It's only right that I do some service for him."

One morning, He asked Dhanna, "Do you have any land?"

Dhanna Jat replied, "I have four acres, but the land is barren. There is no water on that land."

God responded, "Okay, don't worry. I will take care of that."

So God Himself created a well on the barren land. With the water, He cultivated a proper field, the land became fertile, and grew lots of produce.

Dhanna Jat sold the extra crops and his income increased substantially. He asked God, "What should I do with this extra money I receive from the produce?"

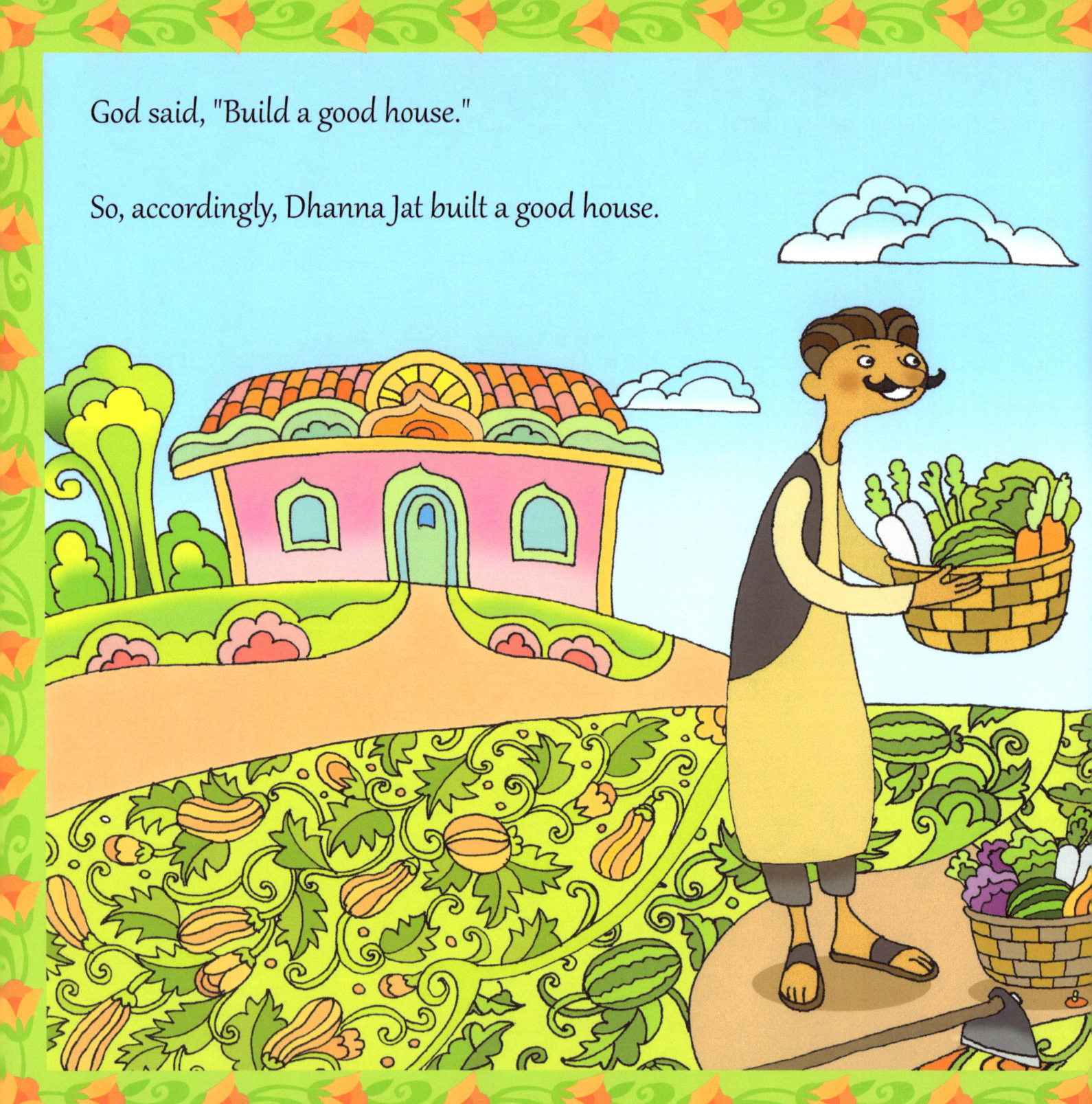

God said, "Build a good house."

So, accordingly, Dhanna Jat built a good house.

The land produced an abundance of food, so much so that Dhanna Jat earned more than he needed and he questioned God what he should do.

God told him, "Buy more land and grow more food."

After awhile, Dhanna Jat's land produced so much food that God told him, "Okay, whatever is surplus food, Dhanna Jat, donate it and begin feeding others."

From that day on, every day about one hundred fifty to two hundred people came to Dhanna Jat's langar that he set up, according to God Almighty's instructions. These people ate at no charge, because the food was from the surplus that grew for Dhanna Jat.

Very quickly a year passed and Trilochan Das returned. He saw the new house, he saw the land where the crops were growing and also saw a new langar. Trilochan Das was quite shocked to see all the development and questioned Dhanna Jat when he saw him.

Dhanna Jat said, "All that has happened is from the deity you gave me. For the first five days, he starved me, but from the sixth day onwards, he has been giving me all this."

Trilochan Das was very curious and asked Dhanna Jat, "Please show me that deity. Who is this person?"

Dhanna Jat replied, "He must've gone to the jungle to fetch wood."

So Trilochan Das ran to the jungle to see this deity. His eyes couldn't believe what he witnessed: wood was automatically being placed on a cart, but there was no one there. This startled Trilochan Das so much that he ran back to Dhanna Jat and stated, "There is nobody there."

Dhanna said, "Maybe He's watering the field. Go there."

Trilochan Das hurried to the field and saw the watermill running on its own, watering the field, and no deity in sight. Again he ran back to Dhanna Jat, who said to Trilochan Das, "In the evening when He comes back, I will speak to Him."

Trilochan Das then requested, "Let me also see Him and take His blessing." Dhanna Jat replied, "I'll speak to Him in the evening and let you know."

In the evening Dhanna met God, Who had manifested in the form of a servant. Dhanna asked Him, "My guru, the family guru, has returned and wants to meet You."

But God told him, "Look, he is not fit for getting my Darshan. So I am not going to give him Darshan."

Dhanna persisted and said, "If You don't give him Your Darshan, then he will feel that I'm just lying about everything that's happening here. So please, I request You to give him Darshan."

He said, "Okay, when you give me food tomorrow, I will give him Darshan for one second."

Dhanna Jat reported to Trilochan Das that, "Tomorrow morning at nine o'clock you will get Darshan."

In the morning, Trilochan Das prepared for his sacred meeting with God. He put a mark on his forehead, eager to make a good impression and arrived an hour early in the attic, where he was to meet God.

At nine o'clock Dhanna's grandmother prepared food, which Dhanna took to the attic, where Trilochan Das was already seated. When Dhanna Jat offered that food, God showed Himself and manifested in the form of a person.

Trilochan Das bent forward to take His blessings, which God gave him, but when Trilochan Das looked up again, God had left.

After Trilochan Das got Darshan from God Almighty Himself in the Form God had taken, he said to himself, "I have been doing this practice for many years and I have never received Darshan before today. But this boy, this Dhanna Jat, has received it."

That humbled Trilochan Das, who bowed down to Dhanna and said, "You are not an ordinary boy."

Dhanna Jat answered, "No, no, all that has happened is because of your deity, which you yourself gave me. That deity made everything happen."

But Trilochan Das disagreed, "No, what you say can't be true, because I have been doing that devotion for a very long time and have gotten nothing."

So it was obvious to Dhanna that Trilochan Das had a big change in attitude. Dhanna Jat accepted what Trilochan Das said and then blessed Trilochan Das and saved his soul.

Therefore, when we do our devotion, we should have true love and faith. If we do our devotion outwardly in a routine manner, then we are not successful.

Whatever devotion we do should be done with as much faith, love and affection for God Almighty or our own Master as we can have.